An Unusual Animal ABC

A IS FOR AXOLOTL

CATHERINE MACOROL

GODWIN BOOKS

Henry Holt and Company
New York

To my family, for being my constant support;
my teachers, who saw potential in me;
my friends past and present, for life lessons;
my editor, for making my vision realized;
my agent, for making this possible;
my publisher, for making my dream come true;
and my niblings, Kasey and Eily,
for giving me the gift of continuous wonder

Henry Holt and Company, *Publishers since 1866*
Henry Holt® is a registered trademark of Macmillan Publishing Group, LLC
120 Broadway, New York, NY 10271
mackids.com

Our books may be purchased in bulk for promotional, educational, or business use.
Please contact your local bookseller or the Macmillan Corporate and
Premium Sales Department at (800) 221-7945 ext. 5442
or by email at MacmillanSpecialMarkets@macmillan.com.

Library of Congress Cataloging-in-Publication Data
Names: Macorol, Catherine, author.
Title: A is for axolotl : an unusual animal ABC / Catherine Macorol.
Description: First edition. | New York: Henry Holt and Company, 2022. | Audience: Ages 4–8 |
Audience: Grades 2–3 | Summary: "A rhyming, ABC adventure picture book that introduces
readers to the most unique animals from around the world"—Provided by publisher.
Identifiers: LCCN 2021029439 | ISBN 9781250108104 (hardcover)
Subjects: LCSH: Animals—Juvenile literature. | Vocabulary—Juvenile literature.
Classification: LCC QL49 .M189 2022 | DDC 590—dc23
LC record available at https://lccn.loc.gov/2021029439

The artist painted individual watercolor swatches and superimposed them into
the illustrations using Adobe Illustrator to create the art for this book.

First Edition, 2022
Printed in China by Hung Hing Off-set Printing Co. Ltd., Heshan City, Guangdong Province

ISBN 978-1-250-10810-4 (hardcover)
5 7 9 10 8 6

ARCTIC OCEAN

NORTH
AMERICA

NORTH
ATLANTIC OCEAN

EUROPE

ASIA

SOUTH
CHINA SEA

PACIFIC
OCEAN

AFRICA

SOUTH
AMERICA

SOUTH
ATLANTIC OCEAN

INDIAN OCEAN

AUSTRALIA

SOUTHERN
OCEAN

ANTARCTICA

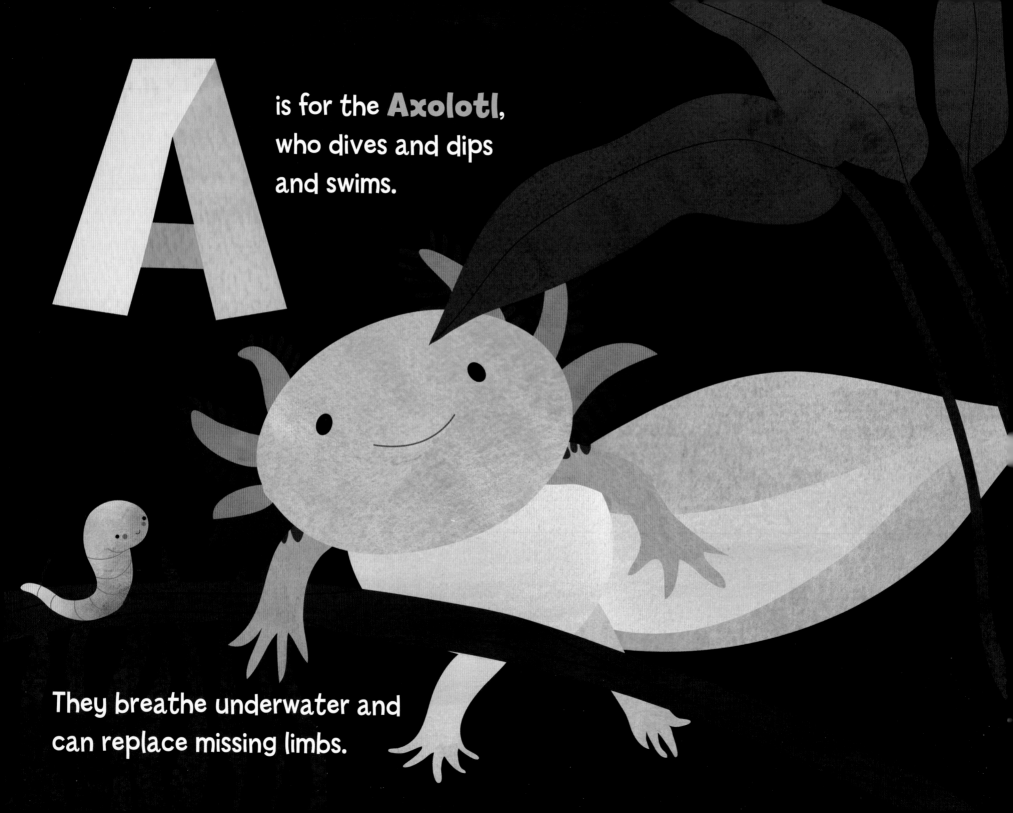

A is for the **Axolotl**, who dives and dips and swims.

They breathe underwater and can replace missing limbs.

B is for the **Binturong**, or bearcat, who's neither bear nor cat.

They smell of buttered popcorn— you can sense them just like that!

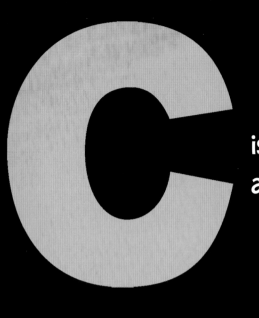

C is for the **Colugo**,
a flying lemur friend.

They glide from tree to tree, from
side to side, from end to end.

D is for a small sea critter, the **Dumbo Octopus.**

They eat their prey whole—nothing's left. They don't share like us!

is for the Echidna, who is a monotreme.

They're mammal, reptile, and marsupial—isn't that extreme?

F

is for the **Fossa**, who lives in Madagascar.

These carnivores' retractable claws can scratch and leave a mean scar.

G is for the Gerenuk,
who eats standing up.

They never need a bit of
water, not even a drop.

H is for the **Hyrax**, cousin to elephants and manatees.

With padded, sweaty feet, these mammals can climb rocks with ease.

is for the **Ibex**, who climbs cliffs on tiptoe.

They will graze the steepest terrain just to avoid snow.

J

is for the **Jerboa**, not quite six inches tall.

But this elusive rodent can jump over a nine-foot wall.

K

is for the **Kiwi**,
a whiskered bird
who cannot fly.

Nostrils on their beaks help them find
food as they go by.

L is for the **Loris**, who looks cute at first sight.

But beware! These slow-moving primates possess a venomous bite.

M

is for the **Maned Wolf**,
a canid oh so chic.

With legs like a doe and a
face like a fox—they are
quite unique.

N is for the **Naked Mole Rat**, who lives underground.

They use their teeth to dig deep tunnels as they move around.

O is for the **Okapi**, related to the giraffe.

They're the best at hide-and-seek and hard to photograph!

P is for the **Pangolin**, who is covered in scales.

Each scale is made of keratin, just like your fingernails.

Q is for the **Quokka**, known for its sweet smile.

Still, don't wake one from a nap or it may turn quite vile.

R is for the **Red Panda**, who loves to eat bamboo.

Giant pandas aren't close relatives, but they're bamboo lovers, too!

S

is for the **Saiga**, known for their migration.

After walking hundreds of miles, these antelopes deserve a long vacation.

T

T is for the **Thorny Dragon**, who eats thousands of ants for lunch.

Using their short, sticky tongues, the dragons munch and munch and munch.

U

is for the
Uakari,
who is
impossible
to miss.

These monkeys mostly
have red faces, like they're
blushing from a kiss.

V is for the **Vaquita**,
about ten left in the sea.

They're the smallest type
of porpoise and the rarest
you can see.

W

is for the **Water Bear**, who thrives in almost any place.

They've survived five mass extinctions and can live in outer space.

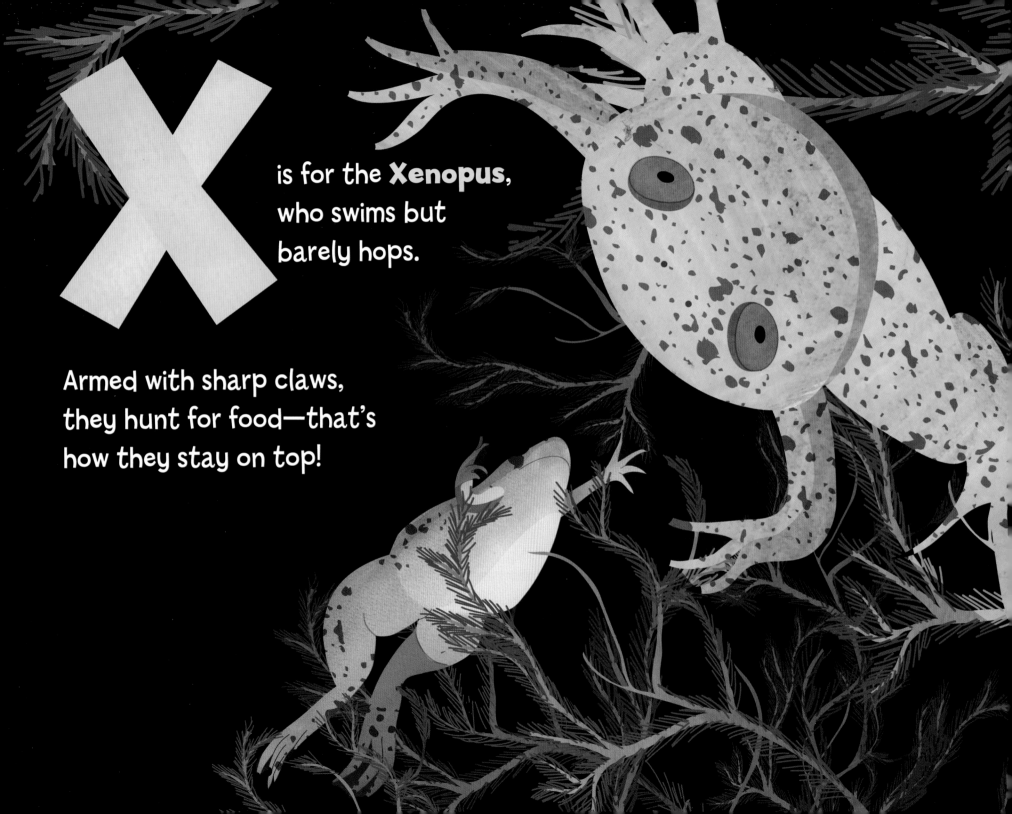

X is for the **Xenopus**, who swims but barely hops.

Armed with sharp claws, they hunt for food—that's how they stay on top!

y

is for the
Yeti Crab,
who mainly
eats bacteria.

They grow it on their
bristly claws, like a
personal cafeteria.

Z is for the **Zebra Duiker**, who tends to run and hide.

But they'll defend their territory, so don't get on their bad side.

Meet the Animals

 Axolotl: Axolotls are unlike other salamanders—they use gills located in their heads to breathe underwater! You can find axolotls in Lake Xochimilco in Mexico. These fascinating creatures are critically endangered.

 Binturong: Despite having a catlike face and a bearlike body, binturongs, also known as bearcats, are neither. This vulnerable animal belongs to the Viverridae family, made up of small- to medium-sized mammals. Binturongs are found in Southeast Asia and are the only viverrids with prehensile tails, used to grasp and hold objects.

 Colugo: Colugos are also known as flying lemurs, but "gliding" lemur might be more accurate. Colugos stretch their skin and glide up to 200 feet between trees in the rainforests of Southeast Asia!

 Dumbo Octopus: If the dumbo octopus brings to mind a certain Disney character, you're on the right track—these octopuses are named after Dumbo the elephant because of their prominent "ears," which are actually fins. The dumbo octopus occupies the waters of New Zealand, Australia, California, Oregon, the Philippines, and New Guinea and can dive 13,000 feet.

 Echidna: Along with platypuses, echidnas belong to a group of egg-laying mammals called monotremes, which were around when dinosaurs still walked the earth. Echidnas live in Australia, Tasmania, and New Guinea and are endangered.

 Fossa: Fossas, measuring nearly five feet, are the largest carnivores in Madagascar. This threatened species is a relative of the mongoose. With their semi-retractable claws and flexible ankle joints, fossas are efficient hunters.

 Gerenuk: Gerenuks are often mistaken for mini giraffes—but the truth is, they're antelopes related to the gazelle. Gerenuks are a near-threatened species found in Africa.

 Hyrax: Hyraxes spend quite a bit of their time sunbathing. They're also known for their "singing," which they use to announce territory, make distress calls, and more. There are three kinds of hyrax: rock, tree, and bush (the yellow-spotted hyrax). They're most commonly found in Africa, but rock hyraxes also inhabit the coast of the Arabian Peninsula.

Ibex: Ibexes are mountain goats that make their homes in the European Alps, Iberia, Central Asia, Northern Africa, and the Caucasus. They climb the steepest cliffs using their segmented and concave hooves.

 Jerboa: Jerboas are elusive rodents that only come out in the evening or at night in Eastern Europe, Africa, and Asia. They use their long whiskers to navigate in the dark. Some species of jerboa are endangered.

 Kiwi: Kiwis are flightless birds with an exceptional sense of smell. They use nostrils on the tips of their beaks and their long whiskers to find food on the forest floors of New Zealand. The kiwi population is in serious decline.

 Loris: Loris means "clown" in Dutch. Lorises have enormous eyes that allow them to see in near-complete darkness. These primates live in Asia.

 Maned Wolf: Maned wolves, also known as foxes on stilts, are neither wolves nor foxes. These grassland canids are found in South America, where their population is near threatened.

 Naked Mole Rat: Naked mole rats live in complex underground colonies in Africa. They have poor eyesight and long, sharp teeth that grow outside their mouths. Despite their name, they're not related to rats—porcupines are a much closer relative.

 Okapi: Okapis are found in the Congo. Sometimes referred to as the "African Unicorn," okapis' brown and white stripes camouflage them perfectly in the dense lowland forests they call home. These animals are endangered.

 Pangolin: Pangolins are the only mammals in the world covered in keratin scales. They love to eat ants and termites—they don't have teeth, but they can consume 20,000 ants and termites in a day using their long, sticky tongues. Eight species of pangolin are split between the continents of Asia and Africa, and while some are vulnerable, others are endangered.

 Quokka: Furry quokkas are located in Australia, mostly on Rottnest and Bald Islands. They've been dubbed the "happiest animals in the world" because they always look like they're smiling. While these vulnerable animals resemble rats, they're most closely related to kangaroos.

Red Panda: Red pandas live in Asia. They're fairly solitary and crespuscular, which means they're most active at dawn and dusk. Fewer than 10,000 red pandas are estimated to remain in the wild due to habitat loss and poaching.

Saiga: Saigas are located in Southeastern Europe and Central Asia. They're best known for their long migrations, which can have them traveling up to 72 miles per day. The saiga's bulbous nose filters out airborne dust during summer migrations and warms cold air during winter migrations. These animals are critically endangered.

Thorny Dragon: Thorny dragons, also known as thorny devils, are covered in spines. They're found in Australia, where their population is threatened due to habitat loss and climate change.

Uakari: Uakaris are small monkeys that live in the rainforest region of South America. They use their powerful legs to jump from tree to tree. Uakaris are considered vulnerable due to habitat loss and hunting.

Vaquita: Vaquitas are the rarest marine mammals. These small cetaceans (whales, dolphins, and porpoises) live in the shallow seas of North America, namely in the northern Gulf of California. It's estimated that there are fewer than 10 left in the wild.

Water Bear: Water bears, also known as tardigrades, are nearly indestructible. They're micro-animals found in North America, Asia, and Europe in extreme environments, including frozen lakes. Water bears can curl into dehydrated balls called tuns and retract their heads and legs. Once soaked in water, they'll be revived.

Xenopus: Xenopuses are among the only amphibians with claws. Unlike most frogs, xenopuses have no tongues, teeth, or vocal sacs. Still, they'll consume just about anything—including their own dead skin. Xenopuses are found in Africa.

Yeti Crab: Yeti crabs have hairlike bristles called setae, which they use to farm microbes and navigate the ocean floor in Antarctica. To keep from freezing, yeti crabs gather around hydrothermal vents.

Zebra Duiker: Zebra duikers, much like real zebras, sport distinct black stripes. These small antelopes are primarily found in the dense rainforests of Africa, and their diets are mostly made up of fruit, grass, and leaves—although they'll sometimes scavenge for meat. They're a vulnerable species.